Way Beyond PowerPoint: Making 21st-Century Presentations™

WRITING
TERM PAPERS
WITH COOL NEW DIGITAL TOOLS

JOE GREEK

D1278720

rosen publishing's
rosen
central®

NEW YORK

Published in 2014 by The Rosen Publishing Group, Inc.
29 East 21st Street, New York, NY 10010

Library of Congress Cataloging-in-Publication Data

Greek, Joe.
Writing term papers with cool new digital tools/by Joe Greek.
    p. cm. —(Way beyond PowerPoint: making 21st century presentations)
Includes bibliographical references and index.
ISBN 978-1-4777-1835-3 (library binding)—
ISBN 978-1-4777-1853-7 (pbk.)—
ISBN 978-1-4777-1854-4 (6-pack)
1. Academic writing – Juvenile literature. 2. Research—Juvenile literature. 3. Report writing—Juvenile literature. I. Greek, Joe. II. Title.
LB1047.3 G74 2014
808—dc23

Manufactured in the United States of America

CPSIA Compliance Information: Batch #W14YA: For further information, contact Rosen Publishing, New York, New York, at 1-800-237-9932.

CONTENTS

INTRODUCTION

It was a Monday like any other Monday, except for the fact that your teacher announced that a term paper assignment would be due in a couple of weeks. You don't have much time to research and write the paper or prepare the oral presentation that will go along with it.

A term paper can sound daunting when you consider all of the work that is necessary to complete it, much less get a high grade. A term paper needs to be able to capture the attention of the audience. At the same time, it must also provide them with clear points and valid information that supports the subject matter and persuades them of the validity of your viewpoint, argument, or thesis. A great term paper also involves a lot of high-quality research, organization, and planning.

In the past, term papers were limited to the technology available to students. So, in most cases, students were only expected to turn in handwritten or typed papers. However, with today's ease of access to computers, the Internet, and free applications, teachers are expecting students to go beyond the confines of text-only productions. Having access to the Internet puts you at the forefront of communicative technology. Various programs available online make it possible to create multilayered term papers that are rich in images, audio, and even video. And most of these tools are free to use!

Access to a computer and the Web is all that today's student needs to begin researching and creating a great term paper.

Another great part about researching, writing, and presenting a term paper with the help of today's technology is that you can access your work from nearly anywhere that has an Internet connection. This makes it possible to work on the project from school, from home, or at the library. In the case of collaborative (or group) research and writing projects, this same technology allows team members to work with each other even when they are in different locations.

As you will see, there is a wide variety of online and offline tools to help you research, write, edit, prepare, and present your term paper. Likewise, there are a wealth of techniques and tips for exactly how to use them most efficiently and effectively.

CHECK YOUR SOURCES!

Your teacher has given you a topic upon which to write a digital term paper. With so much information available online, however, you find yourself wondering where to begin your search and how to organize what you find. When you conduct online research, you invariably discover a world of knowledge about almost any and every topic. Navigating the Web to locate the best sources of information and figuring out how to keep track of your growing body of research are the first steps to writing a great term paper.

WEB SITES YOU CAN TRUST

According to the research organization Netcraft, the number of active Web sites on the Internet has exceeded one billion. As you begin researching your term paper through search engines such as Google, you will discover thousands—if not millions—of Web pages relevant to your topic. In many cases, the first several sites appearing at the top of your search results will come from reliable sources. However, less-than-credible pages often rank high in search results as well. This is why it is important to know how to identify Web sites that have a reputation for providing the most accurate information about your topic.

One of the easiest ways to recognize a reliable page is to look at its Web address or, in technical terms, its uniform resource locator (URL). You should especially pay attention to the last section of the Web address, which tends to be three letters following a period, such as ".com," ".org," ".gov," or ".edu." Web sites that are widely regarded as being the most reliable sources by teachers are those that end with ".gov" and ".edu." These are official government organizations, such as www.cdc.gov (Centers for Disease Control and Prevention), and educational institutions, such as www.harvard.edu (Harvard University). The information you will find on these two types of Web sites has, in most cases, been thoroughly studied, verified, and approved by leading professionals or scholars.

Wikipedia is both a highly useful and a highly controversial online information resource. The site operates as an encyclopedia that contains millions of pages dedicated to individual topics and subtopics. The downside of Wikipedia is that anyone can write and edit the pages found within it, and therefore false information occasionally becomes published. Most teachers frown upon using the site as a source for term papers. Nevertheless, Wikipedia pages can be a great starting point for researching your topic.

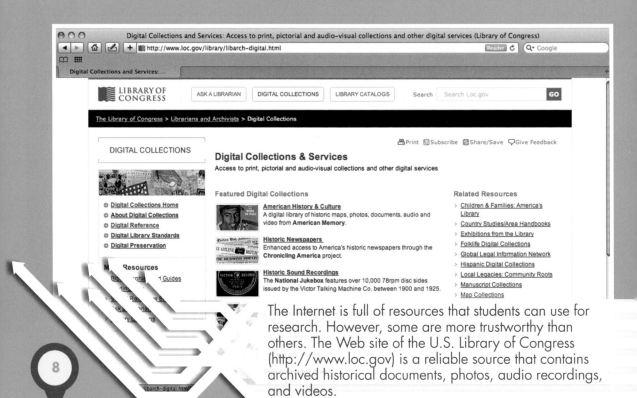

The Internet is full of resources that students can use for research. However, some are more trustworthy than others. The Web site of the U.S. Library of Congress (http://www.loc.gov) is a reliable source that contains archived historical documents, photos, audio recordings, and videos.

As you read a Wikipedia page you will notice small numbers within brackets that float higher than the rest of the text. These numbers are called superscripts. When you click on them, the screen will automatically scroll to a section toward the bottom of the page called "References." These references, in most case, will include links to trustworthy sources, including news articles and government surveys that confirm the information found on the Wikipedia page. Additionally, Wikipedia pages contain a section called "See Also" that contains links to other Web sites related to the topic.

Wikipedia can provide an abundance of information on your topic. Always be sure, however, to double-check the sources that are provided and avoid citing the Wikipedia page itself in your term paper.

RESEARCH ENGINES AND DIGITAL LIBRARIES

The well-known search engines, such as Google, Yahoo!, and Bing, will provide you with thousands, if not millions, of information sources—both reliable and dubious—as you begin to research your topic. Luckily, there are more specialized search engines that show only results from academic and trustworthy sources of online research. Using these search engines helps guarantee that you are finding the best, most trustworthy and accurate information possible.

These academic search engines work the same way that regular search engines do, but they provide links to approved academic journals, government and educational organizations, and online research papers. A few of the most popular of these search engines include:

- **iSeek Education (www.iseek.com):** A search engine of authoritative, editor-reviewed Web pages
- **Directory of Open Access Journals (www.doaj.org):** A large collection of searchable, free academic and peer-reviewed publications and articles

- **Athenus (www.athenus.com):** A search engine for science and engineering-related topics.

Many universities and government organizations in the United States and Canada provide access to large online libraries for research purposes. These libraries contain viewable academic journals, articles, and research papers, as well as digital media such as images and audio and video clips. The U.S. Library of Congress (www.loc.gov) and its Canadian equivalent, Library and Archives Canada (http://www .bac-lac.gc.ca), provide large online collections of documents and media pertaining to the two nations' histories and cultures.

Other great sources of information for your term paper's topic can be found in the free online libraries and archives of universities, including:

- **Digital History (www.digitalhistory.uh.edu):** An interactive collection of historical records, articles, media, and other resources about U.S. history created by the University of Houston
- **Yale University Library (http://digitalcollections.library.yale.edu):** A Searchable archive of historical books, articles, journals, and media that cover a variety of topics
- **University of Cambridge Digital Library (http://cudl.lib.cam. ac.uk):** Features scanned historical documents and writings, including collections from notable figures such as Isaac Newton and Charles Darwin

KEEPING TRACK OF DIGITAL SOURCES

As you find valuable information sources online, you will also want to be able to easily keep track of them as you go through the process of gathering and organizing your research and writing your term paper. Luckily, there are plenty of tools at your disposal to simplify this part of the term paper process.

As you may already know, your Web browser allows you to bookmark pages for later viewing. However, you might not always use the same

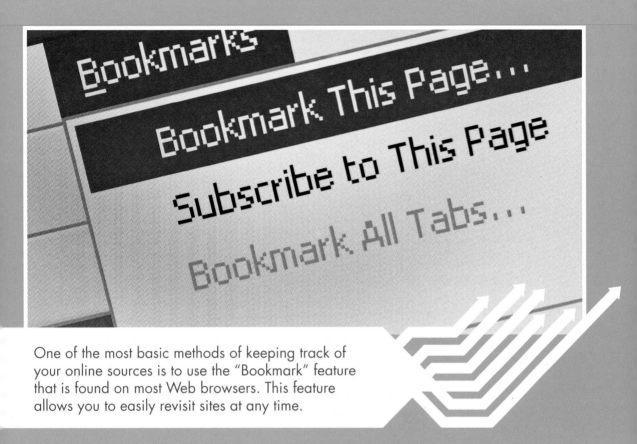

One of the most basic methods of keeping track of your online sources is to use the "Bookmark" feature that is found on most Web browsers. This feature allows you to easily revisit sites at any time.

computer or digital device when researching. Some Web browsers, including Apple's Safari and Google's Chrome, now make it possible for you to view your bookmarks on different devices. To do this, you will need to set up an account with the company that created your preferred Web browser.

For example, after you have set up a Google account, you will be able to log into the Google Web browser Chrome, whether you are using a school terminal, home computer, digital tablet, or even a smartphone. This is called "synching," which basically means that your preferences, bookmarks, and even passwords are stored on the Internet so you can access them from any location. However, when you are using a computer that does not belong to you, remember to log out of the browser when you

ADDING NOTES TO WEB SITES

Wouldn't it be cool if you could use a yellow highlighter on your computer screen to make note of important information related to your term paper? Fortunately, there are online tools that allow you to do just that without damaging your computer. The social bookmarking Web site Diigo offers a user-friendly add-on for most Web browsers that allows you to highlight text and pictures on Web pages. The add-on even makes it possible to add comments anywhere on a Web page so that you can quickly jot down ideas and notes. Another great feature of Diigo is that it allows you to share your marked-up Web pages (displaying your highlights and comments) with other people who also have the Diigo add-on. If you are working on a collaborative term paper or group project, this feature makes it easy to share sources and notes with other team members.

are done so that no one else will have access to your passwords or other personal information after you have left.

If you are unable to access or simply feel uncomfortable logging into a browser on different devices, there are other options that will allow you to access your bookmarks from multiple devices. Social bookmarking Web sites, including services such as Diigo (www.diigo.com) and Symbaloo (www.symbaloo.com), will store your bookmarks online. Simply visit one of these sites, set up an account, and bookmark Web pages that are useful to your project. You will then be able to log into them from any device with a Web connection.

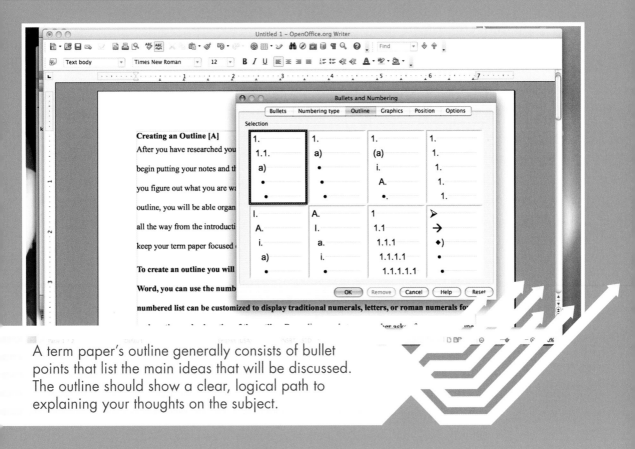

A term paper's outline generally consists of bullet points that list the main ideas that will be discussed. The outline should show a clear, logical path to explaining your thoughts on the subject.

CREATING AN OUTLINE

After you have researched your term paper topic and gathered information sources relevant to it, it is time to begin putting your notes and thoughts together by crafting an outline. A well-designed outline will help you figure out what you want to say throughout your paper—what information you will use, where it will go, and what point it will make or argument it will prove. By structuring your thoughts into an outline, you will be able to organize them in a way that will help to create a smooth flow of information all the way from the introduction to the conclusion. A well-planned outline will help you keep your term paper focused on the most important points of the subject that you are writing about.

To create an outline you will need to use a word processor such as Microsoft Word. Within MS Word, you can use the numbered list feature that is found in the formatting toolbar. A numbered list can be customized to display traditional numerals, letters, or roman numerals for each section and subsection of the outline. Depending on what your teacher asks of you, your outline may contain several different elements. These may include an introduction, transitioning statements, supporting paragraphs, a conclusion, and a summary. When you turn on the numbered list feature, you can begin adding the various elements of your term paper. To create subsections, you can bring your cursor beneath a section and hit the "Increase Indent" button, which is also located within the formatting toolbar.

WORDS ON THE PAGE: WORD PROCESSING BASICS

Once you have researched your topic and created an outline, it is time to begin the actual process of writing the term paper. But before you start writing, you should become familiar with a few of the helpful features that word processors such as MS Word and Google Docs provide. The Web is also full of great resources that you can take advantage of when writing a term paper.

Depending upon the word processor you use to write your term paper, you will have a variety of tools at your disposal. For the most part, however, word processors all have many of the same features, and these are generally organized in a similar fashion. This makes it easy to switch between word processing programs if necessary.

PAGE FORMATTING

In most cases, your teacher will ask you to include page numbers within the paper. To do this, you can go to the drop-down menu called "Insert" at the top of the program. This will give you the option to number each page. Furthermore, you will have the option to place the numbers at the top or bottom of the page—left, right, or center—and to use traditional Arabic numerals (1, 2, 3, 4. . .) or Roman numerals (I, II, III, IV. . .).

If your teacher wants you to add more information to the pages—such as your name, the paper's title, and the date on which you turned your paper in—you can create a "header" or "footer." This option is usually found under the "Insert" menu, but in newer versions of MS Word it can be found under the "Document Elements" menu.

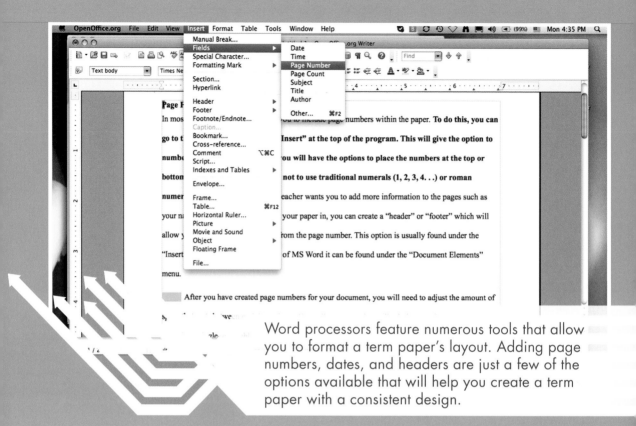

Word processors feature numerous tools that allow you to format a term paper's layout. Adding page numbers, dates, and headers are just a few of the options available that will help you create a term paper with a consistent design.

After you have created page numbers for your document, you will need to adjust the amount of space that exists between each line of text. Generally, your teacher will ask that you format your paper with double spacing. This option is usually found in the "Format" menu under "Line Spacing" or "Paragraph." Within the "Format" menu, you have control over other aspects of the layout of your paper, including the amount of space between the edge of the paper and the text, which can be selected with the "Indent" option.

ADVANCED TEMPLATES

If you plan on incorporating media elements (images, for example) into your term paper, advanced word processors such as MS Word and Apple's Pages provide a variety of templates for you to use. The templates found in these programs can be used to create different types of print media, including brochures, flyers, invitations, and business cards.

For the purpose of a term paper—and depending upon a teacher's requirements for the project—students can use a brochure template to create an eye-catching presentation of text, supporting graphics, and media. In MS Word, the advanced templates feature can be activated by choosing the "Publication Layout" option found underneath the "View" menu.

After selecting a desired template, you can adjust the different elements within the document to better suit your term paper. You can delete sections from the template that don't necessarily suit the purpose of the term paper or its content and style requirements.

WORDS AND GRAMMAR

After you have formatted your document and chosen a template, you can begin the actual writing process. As you put your thoughts to paper, you should take

Using the "Spellcheck" feature in a word processor helps identify potential spelling errors. Additional tools will help you find mistakes in grammar and synonyms that will expand and enrich your word choices.

note of the helpful tools that most word processors include. Many of the most useful features you will use as you write your term paper will be located within the "Tools" menu. The "Word Count" feature, for instance, keeps track of the amount of text you have typed. It can serve as a guide to help you decide how much space can be devoted to each section of a paper when there is a page or word limit to consider.

The "Tools" menu also has several grammatical resources that will define words, check spelling, and suggest synonyms so that you can diversify your word choice. You can also access these options by right-clicking on a highlighted word. Doing this will bring up a small menu near the text from which you can choose an option.

IN-TEXT CITATION AND WORKS CITED PAGE

One of the most tricky parts of writing a term paper is the creation of a works cited (or bibliography) page and providing in-text citation. The works cited page is placed at the very end of a term paper. Its main purpose is to lend credibility to the information in your paper, prove that you put effort into the research, and also give credit to the original sources.

Depending on the type of sources you are referencing, the citations will include various elements such as the author's name, the book or article title, the source's URL or place of publication, the date of publication or posting, and the date the source was viewed or retrieved by you. There are a few different styles of citation that you may use. The two primary styles you will most often encounter as a student are the Modern Language Association (MLA) and American Psychological Association (APA) styles.

Most term papers will also require in-text citations in the body of the term paper. The in-text citations directly follow quotes and information that you have paraphrased from a source. MS Word's "Citations" feature, which can usually be found under the "Insert" menu, reduces the amount of work that is required to create and properly format both of these elements.

ALTERNATIVES TO MICROSOFT OFFICE

MS Word is part of Microsoft's collection of software called Office, which also includes PowerPoint (slide presentation software) and Excel (spreadsheets). The Office suite of programs has become the standard software used by schools and businesses worldwide. However, its price tag often prevents many individuals from being able to use the programs. Fortunately, there are free alternatives when Office is not an option. Google Drive, for one, provides programs that are similar to Office and has the added benefit of online and offline usability.

Better alternatives for offline use, however, are provided by LibreOffice (www.libreoffice.org) and Apache OpenOffice (www. openoffice.org). These two software bundles include nearly identical programs that contain many of the more advanced features found in Office. In addition, they support the same file types that are used by the Office programs, including .doc,.docx, and .pptx.

If you are using MS Word, you can simply fill in the appropriate fields within the "Citations" menu. The program will keep track of your sources and automatically generate a Works Cited page. The feature also lets you insert in-text citations into your paper when they are needed. If you do not have MS Word, there are several Web sites that will also generate properly formatted citations, including EasyBib (www.easybib.com) and Citation Machine (www.citationmachine.net).

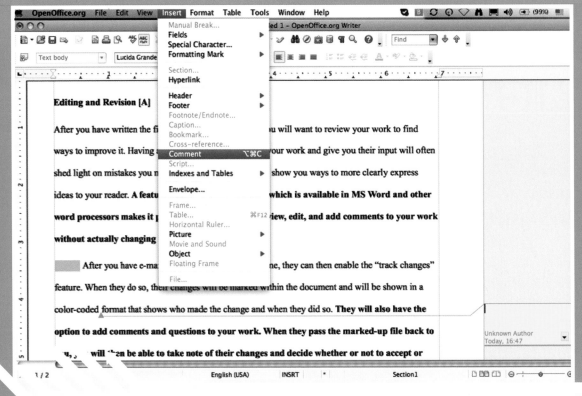

Using the "Track Changes" feature in a word processor allows you or someone who is reviewing your work to add comments, suggestions, and questions that may help you improve your term paper.

EDITING AND REVISION

After you have written the first draft of your term paper, you will want to review your work to find ways to improve it. Having a friend or parent look over your work and give you feedback will often shed light on mistakes you may not have noticed and show you ways to more clearly express ideas to your reader. A feature called "Track Changes," which is available in MS Word and other word processors, makes it possible for others to review, edit, and add comments to your work without actually changing the original wording.

20

After you have e-mailed your term paper to those people who have agreed to review your work, they can then enable the "Track Changes" feature. When they do, their changes will be marked within the document and will be shown in a color-coded format that shows who made the change and when. Your reviewers will also have the option to add comments and questions to the document. When they pass the marked-up file back to you, you will then be able to take note of their changes and decide whether or not to accept or ignore them.

This feature can be especially helpful when you are working on a term paper with another person or in a group. However, it can also be helpful when you, alone, are going over your work and want to leave notes for possible changes that you may wish to revisit and decide upon later on.

GOING MULTIMEDIA: ENHANCING YOUR TEXT

Long gone are the days when term papers were confined to text alone. Today's software and online tools make it possible for students to create media-rich term papers that incorporate visual and audio components that will wow any audience of classmates and teachers. And because these options are now more readily available to students, many teachers are beginning to require that students include these elements in their term papers. In the following sections, we will discuss the different ways you can turn an ordinary term paper into a colorful, dynamic, interactive, and multilayered presentation that will capture the attention of your audience.

IMAGES AND PHOTOGRAPHS

There are several different ways you can go about using images within your term paper. One way—the easiest method—is to simply insert them into your text document. A second way to use media such as images is to create a slideshow to accompany an oral presentation of your term paper.

To find images that relate to your topic, you can use a search engine such as Google. On the Google homepage, click the "Images" tab at the top of the page and enter keywords that relate to your topic in the search bar. As you browse through the image search results, you should look for images that are specifically related to the information or points that your paper discusses. Carefully read the rights and permissions section associated with each image. You may have to obtain

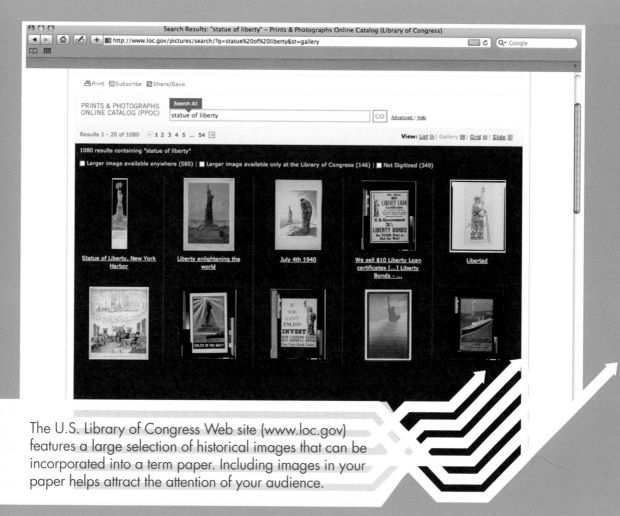

The U.S. Library of Congress Web site (www.loc.gov) features a large selection of historical images that can be incorporated into a term paper. Including images in your paper helps attract the attention of your audience.

permission from the Web site, artist, museum, photographer, or photo agency to use an image in your report or presentation.

Other great resources for finding photographs are public domain (requiring no permission to use) historical archives such as the Library of Congress's Web site. The images found on the LOC site are easily searchable, are available for free download, and often include content-rich information about the photograph or image that you may choose to include in your project. As you find images that would go well with your term paper, save them to a folder on your computer where you will not forget their location.

FINDING WHAT YOU'RE LOOKING FOR

You will be able to find better, more relevant and appropriate archival images, photographs, audio and video files, and other media elements when you narrow down your search, using very specific search parameters and terms. One way to improve your ability to find what you need from a search engine is by knowing how to use keywords to your advantage. Keywords can be found within the text of a Web site or sometimes encoded—but not visibly seen—within an image or multimedia file.

Search engines like Google scan Web sites to find phrases and keywords that match a search query. However, from time to time certain words and phrases will produce multiple unrelated results. For example, if you searched for "Notre Dame" on Google, you would get results relating to both the college in Indiana and the historic cathedral in Paris, not to mention thousands of high schools and churches worldwide. However, if you want to only see image results of the University of Notre Dame's football helmets, you could include the term "helmet." The search engine would first seek out images that include both "Notre Dame" and "helmet," putting those images closer to the top of the results list.

You can also filter results by instructing the search engine to skip over certain sites and files. To reduce specific types of results from showing up in a search, you can add a minus sign (-) directly in front of the keyword you wish to avoid. Referring back to the Notre Dame example, by including "-Paris" within the search, you will filter out most results relating to the famous French cathedral.

Graphs and charts are another set of visual components that can be used in a term paper to draw attention to important data related to a topic. For example, if your topic is about an endangered species, you could create a bar graph that shows the decline of the animal's population over a set number of years. Spreadsheet programs such as MS Excel have easy-to-use tools to make different types of charts and graphs that you can then save and embed within your term paper or place within a presentation slide. The National Center for Education Statistics (http://nces.ed.gov/nceskids/createagraph) offers a free online tool to create different types of charts that you can then save in various file formats to use in your project. However, try to avoid overloading your audience with charts and graphs. Instead, use them only to highlight truly attention-grabbing numbers and statistics.

Once you have picked out and saved images or created graphs and charts for your project, you can then embed them directly into your term paper. With more modern programs, you will be able to simply drag the image onto your document. In some cases, you may have to use the "Insert" menu of the program and locate the image's file location on your computer. As you add your images to the term paper, be sure that you place them close to the text that they are referencing. You should add a caption to the image that describes what is shown and provides a credit to the photographer or Web site from which it was taken. Also, don't go overboard on the use of images in a term paper. Too many images can become a distraction for the reader, and they will become more focused on what they are seeing rather than what they are reading. Too many images may give the impression that you are trying to pad thin content.

HISTORIC RECORDINGS AND AUDIO CLIPS

The use of audio clips can bring the subject of a term paper to life. Imagine letting your audience listen to an actual recording of Martin Luther King Jr.'s historic 1963 "I Have a Dream" speech as opposed to merely quoting or paraphrasing it. Listening to the actual voices and sounds surrounding your subject can develop a connection between your audience and the topic as their minds begin to visualize and interpret what they are hearing.

There are numerous Web sites that contain audio clips of historical speeches and radio broadcasts that you can download or stream over speakers in a classroom setting. The Web sites of many academic institutions and government organizations often host a large variety of free, downloadable audio files that are searchable by subject. Another excellent source is the Library of Congress's Web site, which contains a vast catalogue of downloadable audio clips pertaining to American and world historical events.

Going Digital with Film

Alongside images and audio, incorporating video into a term paper can make your work stand out from the pack. Thanks to the Internet, students have free access to an array of videos that range from U.S. astronauts Neil Armstrong and Buzz Aldrin walking on the moon in 1969 to public service addresses regarding the negative health effects of smoking.

YouTube offers the largest collection of videos available online, which makes it a good place to start searching for videos that are related to your

Creating a video to accompany your term paper will create a longer-lasting impact upon the audience. Visual demonstrations of subjects such as science experiments will help the audience have a better understanding of your topic.

subject. Remember to pay attention to the rights and permissions associated with each video and obtain any necessary authorization before showing or embedding the video as part of your project. As is the case with other forms of media that are available online, the Web sites of educational and governmental organizations are great places to look for rare, often public domain film footage of historical events and people. Another good reason to browse .edu and .gov Web sites is that they don't have the advertisements that often spring up on video streaming sites.

But why use someone else's video when you can make your own? If you have a cellular phone or digital camera, there is a good chance that your device can record a video or take photographs of high quality. Making your own videos or still images to accompany your term paper is a great way to add depth to the project. You can also recruit friends to participate in and help film the video. A good example of how to incorporate your own videos into a term paper about a science topic would be by performing safe outdoor science experiments that can't be performed inside the classroom. After you have recorded a video, you can retrieve and view it at school by e-mailing the file to yourself, hosting it privately on YouTube, or bringing it to class on a portable hard drive.

ATTENTION-GETTING PRESENTATIONS

If one of the requirements for your term paper is to present it or read it aloud in class, you can create a visually compelling slideshow to accompany your presentation. A slideshow presentation is customizable and can include each of the different types of media elements discussed previously—photos and other images, graphs and charts, and audio and video files.

To create a slideshow, you will need to use a presentation program such as Microsoft PowerPoint or Google Presentation. Creating the slideshow is a relatively simple process, but making an effective one will require an ability to organize the slides in an order that matches up well with the content of the oral presentation. Most slideshow programs are simple in layout and are not difficult to get the hang of. You can usually choose a premade template for your

A slideshow will help your audience stay focused on the key points of your oral presentation. Slideshows can incorporate various elements, including text, images, audio recordings, and video.

project, which includes different styles of slide layouts, animated slide-to-slide transitions, and color patterns. In most cases, you will find an option underneath the "Insert" menu to add image, audio, or video files to a slide. You can easily store and view presentations with the widely used .pptx extension from any device by hosting them on Google Drive.

Before you present a slideshow to your class, you should practice giving your presentation at home in order to get used to delivering your spoken material while simultaneously and smoothly moving from slide to slide.

THE GANG'S ALL HERE! DIGITIZING GROUP PROJECTS

Creating a term paper with a partner or group no longer requires that everyone be in the same room at the same time. In fact, it is now possible to collaborate with another person who is located on the opposite side of the world. Online collaborative programs allow individuals to create documents, store them online, and share them with others. Many of today's readily available programs can be accessed from different types of devices—including tablets and smartphones—making working from any location that much easier. There are numerous ways that you can use such programs to collaborate effectively in an online setting.

GOOGLE DRIVE

Possibly the biggest competitor to Microsoft's suite of Office programs is Google Drive. Drive features Google Docs, which contains programs that are very similar to Office's Word, Excel, and PowerPoint software. Drive also offers cloud storage, file sharing, and collaborative editing. While Drive's programs do not offer as many advanced features as MS Office, it makes up for what it lacks through its ability to be used both online and offline. More important, however, is the fact that multiple individuals can easily work on the same documents with Drive.

To use Drive, individuals should create an account with Google. Doing this will also require that the users create an e-mail account with the Google e-mail service Gmail. When you have created an account and are logged into Google, you will be able to access Drive by clicking on its tab, which appears at the top of the Gmail and Google homepages. Once you have accessed Drive, you can then begin to

Google Drive allows you to store and share files online, including text documents, videos, slideshows, and audio recordings. The free service also features word processor, slideshow, and spreadsheet programs that you can share with others and use for collaborative projects.

create different types of files, including text documents, slideshow presentations, and spreadsheets.

After you have created your document, you can invite group members to become collaborators. To do this, you will need to open the document and click the "Share" option within the "File" menu. Next, you will need to type the e-mail addresses of the individuals with whom you are working. You will also have the option to decide whether your collaborators can edit the document or only view it. If you choose to let others edit the work on Drive, their changes will automatically show up within the document.

ONLINE REVIEW AND MARKUPS

A downside of using MS Word is that it was primarily created for offline use. Yet MS Word's track changes and comment features can be very helpful when multiple people are working on the same term paper or project. To take full advantage of the features, though, would require e-mailing the same text file back and forth between people. This can become confusing and problematic if someone accidentally uses an older version of the file.

Google Docs, however, includes a slightly simplified, streamlined, and more user-friendly version of MS's popular markup feature. By using Google Docs, you have the ability to invite other students or even your teacher to review your work and add comments. If you are working on a collaborative document in Google Drive and want to see what other people have changed or added, you can click on the "File" menu and then select the "See revision history" option. This will bring up a box on the right-hand side of the page that will show previous edits of the document by each group member. The changes will also be color coded to show who made a change. If, for some reason, you need to retrieve a previous iteration of the document before certain changes were made, you can select an earlier version and hit "Restore this revision."

Drive is also a versatile option when you find yourself working on a term paper in different locations such as at home, school, and the public library. Because it was designed as a primarily Web-based program, Drive does not require users to download software that works only on certain operating systems. Most Web browsers support Drive and will only require you to log-in to Google in order to use it. Google has created free downloadable applications that allow users to access Drive from smartphones and tablet devices. This can be an especially helpful feature when you are traveling and have a sudden inspiration for your term paper that needs to be documented and saved immediately.

CLOUD STORAGE

Another option for sharing files with group members and having access to them from other locations is provided by cloud storage. Cloud storage services

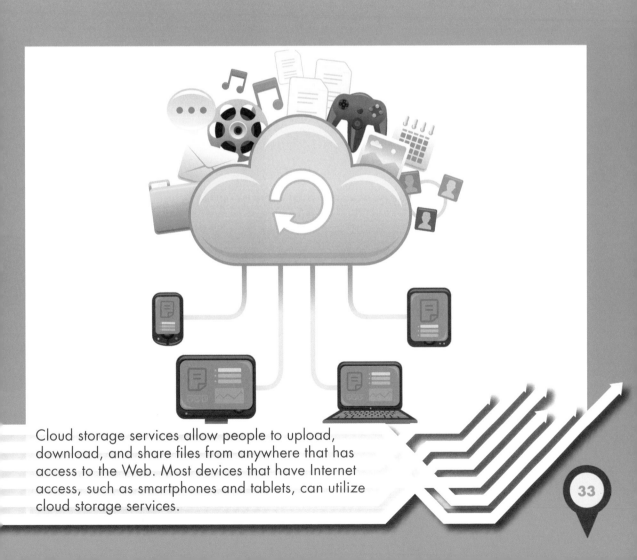

Cloud storage services allow people to upload, download, and share files from anywhere that has access to the Web. Most devices that have Internet access, such as smartphones and tablets, can utilize cloud storage services.

work in much the same way as the hard drive on your computer does. They are essentially off-site storage devices you can upload files to and download files from, via an Internet connection. The stored files are accessible from any device that has an Internet connection.

Google Drive functions as a cloud storage device. Within Drive, you have the option to upload and share most types of files. This is a great capability to have when you are sharing large files such as video or high-resolution photographs that are too big to send via e-mail. Drive provides users with five gigabytes of free cloud storage space, with an option to purchase additional storage. If Drive is not an option for everyone in your group, there are other free cloud storage services, including DropBox (www.dropbox.com).

SKYPE AND VIDEO CONFERENCING

When working collaboratively online, you will occasionally want to discuss ideas and recommendations with each other. Video conferencing is a great way to meet up with your group when you are not at school together. To video

34

Working with a partner or group no longer requires that everyone be in the same location. Video conferencing programs such as Skype gather you and your group together—virtually—without anyone having to leave his or her desk.

conference with a group, your computer or smartphone will need a Webcam and a microphone.

Google provides a free video conferencing service that allows you to interact online with your group in real-time. This Google feature is called Hangouts. It can be accessed from the homepage of Gmail or Google's social network Google+. Simply invite your group members by inputting their e-mail addresses, and they will receive a notification if they are logged into Google. Once everyone has joined a Hangout, you can then discuss the term paper, brainstorm ideas, and assign tasks. Another free alternative to using Hangouts is Skype (www.skype.com), which is owned by Microsoft.

There are a few ways that you and your group can take advantage of video conferencing. First, you will be able to share your ideas and thoughts about your term paper. Second, you can use the screen share option to show everyone what you are currently looking at. This is a helpful way to share your research—including documents, maps, archival images, charts, graphs, photos, and videos. You can then receive immediate feedback while keeping everyone focused on the same discussion.

Finally, video conferencing is particularly helpful when your group has to give an oral presentation of your term paper. You can use it to practice your presentation teamwork and delivery. It can also be used if not every member of the team is present on the day of the presentation. Whoever is not on-site can deliver his or her portion of the presentation remotely via video conferencing. By taking advantage of the digital tools at your fingertips, you will develop the skills and know-how necessary to create and present a grade-A term paper.

ADD-ON An application that can be added to a Web browser to perform various functions.

APPLICATION A program that serves a specialized purpose beyond merely running or operating the computer.

ARCHIVE A Web site that has a collection of viewable records and original documents.

BRAINSTORM To spontaneously contribute ideas in a group setting; to mull over the ideas of an individual or group in order to devise or find a solution to a problem.

BROWSER Software that is used to browse or search the Web and displays Web sites.

COLLABORATE To work on a project with another person or in a group.

CURSOR A movable indicator on a computer screen that is directed by a mouse or touchpad.

EMBED To place something such as a graphic or video into a computer program, file, or Web site.

FILE FORMAT The coding of a file that determines what a computer can do with it or what type of program is needed to run it.

ITERATION A version or incarnation of something that appears in multiple versions.

KEYWORD A word that is entered into a search engine to find specific data or Web sites relevant to the keyword throughout the Internet.

PUBLIC DOMAIN The realm embracing property rights that belong to the community at large, are unprotected by copyright or patent, and are subject to appropriation by anyone; intellectual property, such as writings, photos, videos, and songs, that are free to use by anyone without securing permission or paying for use.

SEARCH ENGINE A Web site or program that finds data and files on the Internet based on inputted keywords and other user settings.

SOFTWARE Programs that control the way a computer operates.

SPREADSHEET A computer file that displays calculations and is used to create lists, tables, and other functions.

SYNCH To share a single set of data among various digital devices (such as a laptop, tablet, and smartphone).

TEMPLATE A file such as a text document or spreadsheet that features a predesigned layout.

UNIFORM RESOURCE LOCATOR (URL) The address of a Web site.

VALID Well-grounded or justifiable; being at once relevant and meaningful; logically correct; appropriate to the end in view; effective.

WORD PROCESSOR A computer program that is used to compose text that can be saved in a digital format.

FOR MORE INFORMATION

American Museum of Natural History
Central Park West at 79th Street
New York, NY 10024-5192
(212) 769-5100
Web site: http://www.amnh.org
The museum houses one of the world's largest and most extensive collections
    of scientific and historical artifacts and exhibits. The Web site includes
    a database of searchable media and articles pertaining to various
    subjects and exhibits.

Encyclopædia Britannica, Inc.
331 North La Salle Street
Chicago, IL 60654-2682
(800) 323-1229
Web site: http://www.britannica.com
Encyclopædia Britannica is an international publisher of educational litera-
    ture. The organization's Web site features a searchable archive of
    information, photographs, and video clips on a variety of topics.

High Tech Kids
111 Third Avenue South, Suite 145
Minneapolis, MN 55401
(612) 781-2203
Web site: http://www.hightechkids.org
High Tech Kids helps kids discover the fun in science, technology, and
    computing.

iD Tech Camps
42 West Campbell Avenue, Suite 301
Campbell, CA 95008
(888) 709-8324
Web site: http://www.internaldrive.com
iD Tech Camps offer summer camps and courses in computing and
    technology.

International Technology Education Association (ITEA)
1914 Association Drive, Suite 201
Reston, VA 20191-1539
(703) 860-2100
Web site: http://www.iteaconnect.org
The International Technology Education Association promotes technology
    education and literacy.

Library and Archives Canada
395 Wellington Street
Ottawa, ON K1A 0N4
Canada
(613) 996-5115
Web site: http://www.bac-lac.gc.ca
Library and Archives Canada is an archive that preserves and makes acces-
    sible the documented history of the country. The collections include
    original documents, archival records, video and audio recordings,
    photographs, and artwork.

Library of Congress
101 Independence Avenue SE

Washington, DC 20540-1400
(202) 707-9779
Web site: http://www.loc.gov
The Library of Congress is a governmental organization that serves as a
     research archive for the U.S. Congress. The Web site features a
     searchable database of original documents, images, and files.

Media Smarts
950 Gladstone Avenue, Suite 120
Ottawa, ON K1Y 3E6
Canada
(613) 224-7721
Web site: http://mediasmarts.ca
MediaSmarts is a Canadian not-for-profit charitable organization for digital
     and media literacy. Its mission is to provide children and youth with the
     critical thinking skills necessary to engage with media as active and
     informed digital citizens.

National Center for Education Statistics (NCES)
Institute of Education Sciences
1990 K Street NW, 8th and 9th Floors
Washington, DC 20006
(202) 502-7300
Web site: http://nces.ed.gov/nceskids
The NCES is a U.S. government organization that collects, analyzes, and
     publishes data on public school financial information. The "Kids' Zone"
     portion of the NCES Web site provides students with information about
     schools, tips on picking a college, educational games, and free online
     tools to create graphs.

Project Gutenberg Literary Archive Foundation
809 North 1500 West
Salt Lake City, UT 84116
Web site: http://www.gutenberg.org
Project Gutenberg is a volunteer organization that digitizes and archives
    culturally important works of literature. The Web site offers more than
    forty-two thousand proofread ebooks that are free to download.
    Books in the archive span most genres, including classic fiction and
    nonfiction works.

WEB SITES

Due to the changing nature of Internet links, Rosen Publishing has developed
an online list of Web sites related to the subject of this book. This site is
updated regularly. Please use this link to access the list:

http://www.rosenlinks.com/WBPP/Term

FOR FUTHER READING

Baule, Steven M., and Julie E. Lewis. *Social Networking for Schools*. Santa Barbara, CA: Linworth, 2012.

Cefrey, Holly. *Researching People, Places, and Events* (Digital and Information Literacy). New York, NY: Rosen Publishing, 2009.

Dixon, Brian. *Social Media for School Leaders: A Comprehensive Guide to Getting the Most Out of Facebook, Twitter, and Other Essential Web Tools*. San Francisco, CA: John Wiley & Sons, Inc., 2012.

Fogarty, Mignon. *Grammar Girl Presents the Ultimate Writing Guide for Students*. New York, NY: Henry Holt & Co., 2011.

Furgang, Kathy. *Netiquette: A Student's Guide to Digital Etiquette* (Digital and Information Literacy). New York, NY: Rosen Publishing, 2010.

Goldenberg, Phyllis. *Writing a Research Paper: A Step-by-Step Approach* (Sadlier-Oxford Student Guides). New York, NY: Sadlier-Oxford, 2004.

Hanley, Victoria. *Seize the Story: A Handbook for Teens Who Like to Write*. Fort Collins, CO: Cottonwood Press, 2008.

Harvey, Gordon. *Writing with Sources: A Guide for Students*. 2nd ed. Cambridge, MA: Hackett Publishing, 2008.

Kellner, Hank. *Write What You See: 99 Photos to Inspire Writing*. Fort Collins, CO: Cottonwood Press, 2009.

Learning Express Editors. *Writing in 15 Minutes a Day: Junior Skill Builder*. New York, NY: Learning Express, 2008.

Merrill, Douglas C., and James A. Martin. *Getting Organized in the Google Era: How to Stay Efficient, Productive (and Sane) in an Information-Saturated World*. New York, NY: Crown Business, 2011.

Prentice Hall. *Prentice Hall Writing and Grammar: Communication in Action*. Upper Saddle River, NJ: Prentice Hall, 2008.

Raimes, Ann. *Grammar Troublespots: A Guide for Student Writers*. 3rd ed.

Cambridge, MA: Cambridge University Press, 2004.

Strausser, Jeffrey. *Painless Writing* (Barron's Painless). Hauppauge, NY: Barron's Educational Series, Inc., 2009.

Strunk, William, and E. B. White. *The Elements of Style*. White Plains, NY: Longman, 2008.

Wilkinson, Colin. *Mobile Platforms: Getting Information on the Go* (Digital and Information Literacy). New York, NY: Rosen Publishing, 2011.

Wilkinson, Colin. *Twitter and Microblogging: Instant Communication with 140 Characters or Less* (Digital and Information Literacy). New York, NY: Rosen Publishing, 2011.

Winkler, Anthony C., and Jo Ray McCuen-Metherell. *Writing the Research Paper: A Handbook*. 7th ed. Belmont, CA: Wadsworth Publishing, 2009.

BIBLIOGRAPHY

Agosto, Denise E., and June Abbas. *Teens, Libraries, and Social Networking: What Librarians Need to Know* (Libraries Unlimited Professional Guides for Young Adult Librarians Series). Santa Barbara, CA: Libraries Unlimited, 2011.

Baker, Jack Raymond, and Allen Brizee. "Writing a Research Paper." Purdue Online Writing Lab, February 21, 2013. Retrieved April 2013 (http://owl.english.purdue.edu/owl/resource/658/01).

Butler, Allison. *Majoring in Change: Young People Use Social Networking to Reflect on High School, College, and Work* (Minding the Media: Critical Issues for Learning and Teaching). New York, NY: Peter Lang Publishing, 2012.

Deal, Terrence E., Ted Purinton, and Daria Cook Waetjen. *Making Sense of Social Networks in Schools*. Thousand Oaks, CA: Corwin, 2012.

Dulworth, Michael. *The Connect Effect: Building Strong, Professional, and Virtual Networks*. San Francisco, CA: Berret-Koehler Publishers, 2008.

Handley, Ann, and C. C. Chapman. *Content Rules: How to Create Killer Blogs, Podcasts, Videos, Ebooks, Webinars (and More) that Engage Customers and Ignite Your Business*. Hoboken, NJ: Wiley, 2012.

Hayden, Kellie. "Successful Middle School Research Paper Tips." Suite 101, January 19, 2009. Retrieved April 2003 (http://suite101.com/article/tips-for-successful-middle-school-research-paper-a89794).

Jenkins, Henry, Sam Ford, and Joshua Green. *Spreadable Media: Creating Value and Meaning in a Networked Culture*. New York, NY: NYU Press, 2013.

Lalwani, Puja. "Research Paper Topics for Middle School." Buzzle.com, September 22, 2011. Retrieved April 2013 (http://www.buzzle.com/articles/research-paper-topics-for-middle-school.html).

Lih, Andrew. *The Wikipedia Revolution: How a Bunch of Nobodies Created the World's Greatest Encyclopedia.* New York, NY: Hyperion, 2009.

Purdue Online Writing Lab. "MLA Style." Retrieved April 2013 (http://owl.english.purdue.edu/owl/section/2/11).

Rourke, John T., Ralph G. Carter, and Mark A. Boyer. "How to Write Term Papers." McGraw-Hill Student Success. Retrieved April 2013 (http://novella.mhhe.com/sites/0079876543/student_view0/research_center-999/research_papers30/how_to_write_term_papers.html).

Study Guides and Strategies. "Organizing and Pre-writing: Seven Stages of Writing Assignments." Retrieved April 2013 (http://www.studygs.net/writing/prewriting.htm).

TeachThought.com. "100 Search Engines for Academic Research." November 24, 2012. Retrieved April 2013 (http://www.teachthought.com/technology/100-search-engines-for-academic-research).

Watkins, S. Craig. *The Young and the Digital: What the Migration to Social Network Sites, Games, and Anytime, Anywhere Media Means for Our Future.* Boston, MA: Beacon Press, 2010.

INDEX

ABOUT THE AUTHOR

Joe Greek is a writer who lives in Brooklyn, New York. It was during his years as a middle school student that the Internet started to become more prevalent in homes and schools. Having grown up with the Internet, technology has played a pivotal role in his educational and professional lives. He believes, however, that a healthy balance between living offline and online is necessary in order to succeed in today's evolving culture.

PHOTO CREDITS

Cover © iStockphoto.com/AtnoYdur; p. 5 PhotoAlto/Alix Minde/Getty Images; p. 11 © iStockphoto.com/tomeng; pp. 13, 16, 17, 20 Apache, Apache Foo, Foo, and the Foo logo are trademarks of The Apache Software Foundation. Used with permission. No endorsement by The Apache Software Foundation is implied by the use of these marks; pp. 26–27 Hill Street Studios/Blend Images/Getty Images; p. 29 © Cleve Bryant/PhotoEdit; p. 31 Google and the Google logo are registered trademarks of Google Inc., used with permission; p. 33 iStockphoto.com/Thinkstock; pp. 34–35 © AP Images; cover and interior graphics (arrows) © iStockphoto.com/artvea.

Designer: Nicole Russo; Photo Researcher: Amy Feinberg